The Seven Hills of Rome: The History and Legacy
Heart of the Eternal City

By Charles River Editors

Gaspar Alves' picture of the Piazza del Campidoglio on top of Capitoline Hill

## About Charles River Editors

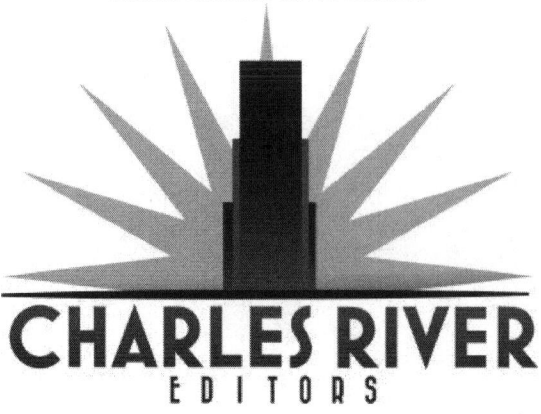

**Charles River Editors** is a boutique digital publishing company, specializing in bringing history back to life with educational and engaging books on a wide range of topics. Keep up to date with our new and free offerings with [this 5 second sign up on our weekly mailing list](), and visit [Our Kindle Author Page]() to see other recently published Kindle titles.

We make these books for you and always want to know our readers' opinions, so we encourage you to leave reviews and look forward to publishing new and exciting titles each week.

# Introduction

**A Good Shepherd fresco from the Catacombs of San Callisto**

## The Seven Hills of Rome

"Rome was a poem pressed into service as a city." In that short line, Anatole Broyard, a 20th century American writer, compactly captures the timeless and enchanting beauty that resides within the Eternal City of Rome. This tourist destination is often one of the highest ranked on bucket lists, for how could one not want to experience its marvelous ruins, mirror-like rivers, and spectacular stretches of aqueducts firsthand? As one sips on fine Italian wine on a terrace overlooking the grand remnants of the Colosseum, one can practically hear the roars of the battling gladiators and the raucous applause of the spectators. And as one strolls through the coarse, yet quaint cobblestone streets, one can almost hear the galloping horses and screeching wheels of chariots in the distance, and even feel the brush of the breeze as they charge past. It is difficult not to fall in love with a city so effortlessly nostalgic it verges on utopian.

The ambitious and fearless emperors that built the legendary Roman Empire from scratch, the broad-shouldered and bronzed gladiators with their iconic plume helmets and glinting swords, and elaborate parties attended by toga-wearing Romans fueled by alcohol, violence, orgies, and other godless acts all paint a picture of Roman life. Indeed, many people are well-versed with these unique scenes of Roman history, but few are familiar with the equally riveting years preceding the dawn of the Roman Republic, and even less people are acquainted with the fabled Seven Hills sitting east of the Tiber River – the core geographical components of Rome, and the very foundations that the Eternal City was built on.

*The Seven Hills of Rome: The History and Legacy of the Hills that Form the Heart of the Eternal City* takes a trek around each and every one of the famous hills, and illustrates how the different events that transpired on each mound has contributed to the shaping of Roman history. Along with pictures depicting important people, places, and events, you will learn about the Seven Hills of Rome like never before.

The Seven Hills of Rome: The History and Legacy of the Hills that Form the Heart of the Eternal City

About Charles River Editors

Introduction

   The Rise of Rome

   Palatine

   Aventine

   Capitoline

   Esquiline

   Quirinal, Caelian, and Viminal

   Online Resources

   Bibliography

Free Books by Charles River Editors

Discounted Books by Charles River Editors

## The Rise of Rome

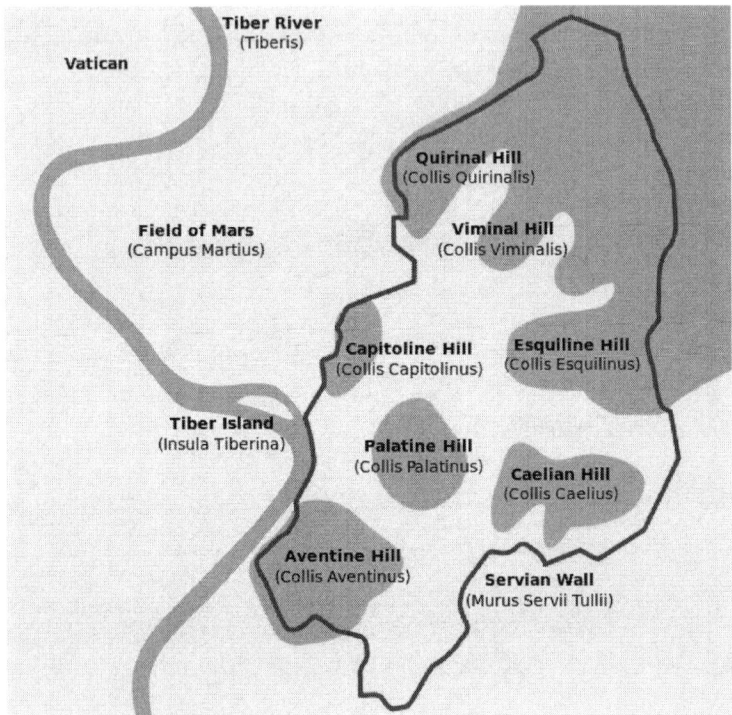

**A map of the hills**

"The populace like the sea is motionless in itself, but stirred by every wind, even the slightest breeze." – Livy, 1st century BCE historian

An assortment of Italic tribes had been occupying the boot of Italy long before the rise of the Romans. The bulk of these people hailed from the lands north of the Adriatic Sea, gradually moving in to the unoccupied nooks and crannies of the peninsula over the years. A fraction were Greek nomads who sailed from their motherland, docking by the shores of southern Italy. Historians described these tribes as primitive and "scarcely civilized," but these settlers, who relied mostly on their flock, would become the very first to crack into the rough earth of never-before-cultivated Italian soil. For the most part, these tribes rarely strayed from familiar territory, for conversing with one another was another struggle in itself; each spoke a crude blend of Aryan and Indo-European languages.

4 tribes composed of what is now referred to as the "Italic race" made up the majority of the population – the Latins, the Sabellians, the Oscans, and the Umbri. The Latins were predominantly in central Italy, living in villages throughout and encircling the Old Latium region, which sat between Mount Circeo and the Tiber River, as early as the late Bronze Age (1200-900 BCE). Latin villagers lived in clusters of "straw-thatched" huts, which later expanded to settlements on the Alban Hills southeast of Rome. When the city erected defensive walls in later years, many of these villages blossomed into cities, bound together by a common language and their worship for Jupiter, the supreme Roman god of light and sky.

The Sabellians, often depicted as a fierce and warmongering people, lived to the south and east of their Latin and Oscan neighbors by the Appenine Range. Since green thumbs were a rarity among the Sabellians, the villagers banked on their livestock, or the booty obtained from looting the harvests of nearby villages for sustenance.

The Oscans, who inhabited the lands southward of the Old Latium, were also quick to grab their spears. They shared many customs with the Latin tribes, but lagged a step behind when it came to agricultural methods, technological innovations, and the general advancement of their society. Many of their descendants, such as the Volscians, Aequians, and Hernicans, would later engage skirmishes with the Romans.

The Umbri were supposedly the oldest of all Italic tribes. The spelling of the original name, "*Ombrii*," which translates to the "people of the thunderstorm," was given to them by the Greeks, for the Umbri were believed to have survived the "Deluge," their take on the divine flood. Umbri communities constructed some of the land's first temples in rural areas, devvoted to Minerva, Clitumnus, Feronia, and other Umbrian deities. The Eugubian Tablets, recovered centuries later, revealed carvings written in the ancient Umbrian language that hinted at animal sacrifices and other early religious rituals. Despite their seniority over the tribes, they would become overwhelmed during later Roman invasions, and either broke up into even smaller villages or merged with nearby communities.

Much of the birth and development of early Rome, however, is indebted to an advanced people that lived northwest of Old Latium known as the "Etruscans." The Etruscan community, which existed between the 8$^{th}$ century and the 2$^{nd}$ century BCE, had a culture largely molded by the Greek presence in Italy, and it was certainly a powerful entity. At one point in time, the Etruscans, a "loose confederation of city-states" to the north of Rome, were guarded by the most robust fortifications on the land, with their territories encompassing lands around the Po to the Tiber Rivers at its prime.

The Etruscans had not only mastered the cultivation of their lands, dipping their toes into commerce only fed their expansion. Instead of sitting on their rich abundance of mineral resources, the Etruscans capitalized on their supplies and created a booming market through manufacture and trade. Specializing in iron, fast-talking Etruscan merchants reeled in traders from not only nearby cities, but Mediterranean powers such as the Phoenicians and the Greeks, Baltic lands, Egypt, and other cultures classified under the Near East. In exchange for locally-sourced iron and other metal products, Etruscans received amber from the Baltic; ivory goods, decorated ostrich eggs, jewelry fashioned out of glass paste, bronze boats, and bejeweled scarabs from Egypt, Sardinia, and other cultures of the Near East; as well as pottery and other handmade artifacts from Greece. Business was so good that the Etruscans minted their own gold and silver coins.

It was through frequent trade with the Greeks and other exotic cultures that these foreign elements became infused into Etruscan culture. For starters, they spoke a language entirely different from other Italic tribes, with an alphabet inspired by a variant of the Greek language and supported by a West Semitic writing system. Also like the Greeks, the Etruscans were polytheistic, and paid tribute to a trio of gods and goddesses – Tin, the sky god; Uni, his wife; and the earth goddess, Cel. Grecian gods, such as Menrva (Minerva), Pacha (Dionysus), and Aritimi (Artemis) were later incorporated into the Etruscan belief system.

Some historians believe that the Etruscans, a highly superstitious people, might have originated from Asia Minor, particularly due to their practice of augury. Augury was fortunetelling, a divine reading of the will of the gods through bird-watching, or the investigation of animal viscera. Other archaeologists have detected traces of Asian culture in some of their ancient language, their trademark pointed shoes, and their love for arches.

Either way, this early melting pot of a tribe descended upon and captured the walled Italic cities of Rome midway through the 7th century BCE, taking the constellation of unrefined clay huts with patchy straw roofs and marrying them to create a unified city – one that would soon become an indomitable force of an empire.

It would only be a matter of time before Roman civilization, which bordered Etruscan territory, absorbed its culture. To begin with, Roman religion, much like that of the Etruscans, revolved around an array of gods and goddesses who could be swayed into interfering with human affairs through sacrifice and other religious rituals. Roman pagans themselves more than dabbled in augury; their priests also possessed sacred texts disclosed to them by the gods and Etruscan sages.

The Etruscan language is also considered an ancestor of the Latin tongue. In fact, Latin has lifted quite a few words straight out of the Etruscan books, such as *"fasces,"* a weapon carried by magisterial attendants featuring an ax blade projecting from a bundle of elmwood, and the *"toga palmata,"* a magistrate's robe. Wealthy Romans of the time understood the significance of Etruscan education, and enrolled their children in both Etruscan and Greek institutes.

Etruscan culture would also leave its enduring imprints on the societal and Christian cultures of Rome. Gladiators brawling until only one was left standing during the funerals for Etruscan nobles was a custom that would later become one of the most distinguishable earmarks of ancient Roman tradition. Depictions of Christian demons and fallen angels were said to have resembled Etruscan demons, and early Roman art and literature were also said to have been heavily seasoned with Etruscan elements.

Most pivotal of the Etruscan influence on Roman civilization was their impact on the infrastructure of the villages, as well as the molding of the Roman governing system and its political values. Before the arrival of the Etruscans, the major settlements on the 7 hills of Rome – the Palatine, Aventine, Campidoglio, Esquiline, Quirinal, Viminal, and Caelian Hills – were cordoned off by their borders and conflicting customs, and as a result, mostly kept to themselves. That was, until the Etruscans introduced an annual region-wide festival that would bring the previously hesitant inhabitants of all hills together.

The *Septimontium* was not only the name of the complex of villages sprinkled throughout the 7 "*montes,*" it also referred to the religious festival all the villagers participated in. Due to the time frame, little information has survived about these celebrations. Chroniclers believe the villagers gathered to pay homage to Apollo, the "Laurel-bearing sun god" with chariot races, plays, and sacred tokens of the people's gratitude. Following an animated procession enlivened by singing, dancing, and other forms of merriment around the Palatine and Esquiline Hills, the villagers convened at the former hill for a special sacrifice. Authorities cleared out large sections of the streets and forbade the use of chariots and other vehicles to make room for the procession. The sacrifice, known as a "*palatuar,*" was conducted by a "bare-headed" pagan priest they called the "*flamen palatualis.*"

Offering "sparkling grains of pure salt" and the "mate of a woolly ewe" slain and neatly gutted by the sacrificial butcher (*agones),* as well as other symbolic gifts, the villagers hoped for blessings of good weather and bountiful harvests from the gods. Other reports of gifts given include gilded statues, such as an ox and a pair of goats for Apollo, and a heifer for Apollo's mother, Leto. Afterwards, some Roman emperors presented senators and knights with baskets brimming with loaves of bread and hunks of meat; miniature versions of these baskets were also doled out to the masses. The festival of the *Septimontium* would become a staple pagan festival that Roman Christians would later adamantly refuse to partake in.

Arguably the most successful of the *Septimontium* team-building activities were the series of games developed especially for the festival, known as the "*Ludi Apollinares,*" or the "Apollo Games." These games were said to have been paid for through taxes acquired from village treasuries, and donations fished from the public. These games took up the majority of the festival's repertoire. They included the *Ludi Scaenici,* a collection of religious plays, mimes, and dances dedicated to the sun gods, the *Ludi Circenses,* the spirited chariot races (later held in the Circus Maximus), and running races, wrestling matches, and other recreational tests of skill. Livy, a Roman historian from the 1st century BCE, summed up the bustling atmosphere of the

*Septimontium* festival: "All the people took part in them [wore] wreaths of flowers. The married women offered prayers. The doors to the houses were opened, meals eaten in the open, and the day marked with every observance..."

It was supposedly through the *Septimontium* that the villages on the hills learned to work as a cohesive unit. The villagers collaborated to drain the low-lying marshy grounds between the hills to the best of their abilities. They transformed these uninhabitable and "malarial" lands into markets where all the villagers could trade, which only strengthened the trust and new political bridges built between these villages. Through the guidance of the Etruscan elite, which instilled in them the concept of a monarchy and the tools to build this centralized form of government, the scattered villages of Rome were soon compressed into one city.

Rome emerged as an official city-state of its own under Etruscan rule. They were buttressed by an initially modest, but soon-to-be stellar military, with much of the training and battle techniques passed onto them by the Etruscans. During spells of strife and dances with disaster, the villagers, now citizens under the same government, learned to pool their resources together to aid their fellow countrymen.

The Etruscans are also credited with planting the seeds for what Rome would become most recognizable for: the structurally sound and phenomenal urban infrastructure seemingly eons ahead of its time. The city's aqueducts, underground sewer system, public baths, smooth stone roads, and durable bridges were said to have been modeled after Etruscan blueprints. The Etruscans also helped to boost Roman trade, and discovered ways to enhance the fields of agriculture and the local metal production.

By the $5^{th}$ century BCE, Rome had landed on the map as one of the mightiest and most influential cities in all of Old Latium, and ironically, all the assistance and resources the Etruscans had parted with would ultimately contribute to their own demise. The Roman armies grew more potent and were soon assertive enough to conquer the last of its neighbors, thereby enlarging the republic.

Once they had triumphed in convincing the Latin villagers to revolt against its leaders and join forces with the republic, the Romans homed in on the Etruscans, whom historians say "lacked a strong national identity." As enterprising as the Etruscans were, those envious of them found a crucial flaw in the disorganization of the multiple governments within Etruria. Some cities were guarded by scores of soldiers, but a large chunk of them were untrained and barely older than the armors on their bodies. While other Etruscan cities had managed to get their hands on veteran troops, they were outnumbered by Greek and Roman soldiers, many of the latter trained by the Etruscan veterans themselves.

In 506 BCE, an alliance of Latins and Greeks from Cumae in South Italy, their biggest competitor in sea power and commerce, conquered Etruscan troops. The Etruscans, gravely crippled, were left vulnerable to being squeezed out of the trade routes on both land and sea. Before long, the reins to the Romans had also slipped from the Etruscan grasp. By 400 BCE, Rome had become an independent institution, rebranded itself as the "Roman Republic," and could now prepare themselves for the next phase of their growth: conquest.

Under the republic, citizens chose representatives to serve as their voice in government. All male descendants of the original settlements were granted full rights as free citizens. Instead of carrying around an identification tucked away in their wallets, ancient Romans wore cream togas to set themselves apart from slaves. These men were permitted to take a freeborn wife, engage in trade, vote, and run for office if they pleased. Below them were half-citizens, mostly the women, who required "guardianship." They were granted partial rights, but were prohibited from trading, casting ballots, or taking a swing at public office. On the same level was a citizen who could hold both a merchant's and voter's license, but were banned from office or wedding freeborn women. Dead last on the tier were the slaves of Roman society, who could only dream of any of these rights.

When the Roman crowns were driven out of town following the rise of the republic, the Roman Senate, which began as a board of 100-300 advisers for the Roman kings, emerged as the sole governor of the independent city. With the sovereigns gone, the position of head of state was replaced with a panel of principal executives known as "consuls." Most consuls and senators were highly-educated noblemen proficient in the skills of persuasion and debate, which they used to talk their peers into their causes. The Senate was also charged with the treasury and financial affairs of the republic, as well as the negotiation of all treaties, and the maintenance and dispatching of troops.

The drafting, revision, and publishing of laws transpired in the Curia, among the most impressive and imposing buildings in the Roman Forum, a rectangular compound of government buildings based in the heart of Rome. In 449 BCE, consuls gathered for the revealing of a new milestone, the 12 Tables. These were the first Roman laws carved by officials into a dozen stone tablets, making it the first constitution literally set in stone. While these commandments guaranteed equality for all free men, most of these unforgiving laws would make even the most hardened souls today flinch at its severity. One controversial law declared, "Quickly kill...a dreadfully deformed child." Another asserted, "If any person has sung or composed against another person a song such as was causing slander or insult to another, he shall be clubbed to death."

Immediately after the debilitating blow the republic suffered following an invasion from the Gauls in 390 BCE, authorities rolled up their sleeves and set out to beef up defenses. Taxes were bumped up to fund a new project, and the Romans went about constructing a wall of stone blocks that would surround the 7 hills of Rome. These defensive walls were dubbed the "Servian Wall" after the 6th king of Rome, Servius Tullius, who was possibly of Etruscan origin. Outside of the wall, a deep trench was excavated for added protection. On the opposite end of the wall was a mountain of the dirt, earth, and rubble dug out for the trench, piled up against the barrier to keep it upright. With the new walls ringing the unified settlements on the 7 hills, authorities received the added benefit of issuing a toll to anyone who used the ford (a shallow strip of river where people could walk across safely).

**Salvatore Falco's picture of a preserved part of the Servian Wall**

**A picture of the Porta Esquilina, a gateway in the Servian Wall.**

The decline of the Roman Republic in the wake of various civil wars triggered the advent of the Roman Empire. When the empire's borders surpassed the length of the Servian Walls, the barrier was retired and substituted with the Aurelian Walls. The new, prolonged defensive walls were made out of brick, and they came complete with square watchtowers and a secret passageway that allowed soldiers to reach a safe point discreetly when under duress.

### Palatine

"Rome was not built in one day." – attributed to English playwright John Heywood

The Palatine, or Palatium Hill, is the oldest and most renowned of the 7 hills. The crown and namesake of its 3 summits (the Palatine; the Germalus, which sat north of the hill; and the Velia, which sat on a low-lying isthmus between the Esquiline and Palatine) was a lush and fertile haven that ached to grow wild with flowers, shrubs, trees, and other greenery, and it attracted gentle critters of all sizes. It is sandwiched between the Circus Maximus and the Roman Forum, the grand structures bathed in the comforts of its shadow under the sweltering heat of the sun. It was once home to the emperors and the most affluent Romans, but what truly distinguishes the hill from the rest is the origin story of its first settlement, as it is one enveloped in the fog of myth and legend.

Evander, the brilliant but temperamental grandson of the Titan and prince of Arcadia, Pallas, was said to have been so hell-bent on control that he murdered his own father for the crown. His mother tugged at his strings with ease, which only made him pounce on his rash decisions that much more. Unfortunately for Evander, his plan backfired; he had hoped to clear his path to the throne, but it was now teeming with the infuriated public, their quivering fingers aimed at the door. Backed into a corner, Evander packed up his belongings and headed off to Italy.

The roaming rogue eventually fell smitten with one majestic hill, which saluted him from the center of the range. Accompanied only by a small band of Arcadian warriors who had defected with him, Evander and his men proceeded to push out the native residents up and down the hill who had been living there as early as the 10th century BCE to make space for a settlement of their own. This new town was called the "Palatine," which was named after his grandfather, or his darling daughter or son, who both shared the genderless name.

The straw huts on the hill were razed to the ground and the site furnished with freshly-constructed stone homes of varying sizes. New residents, many of them of Greek background, occupied the hill in droves, among them the lionized demigod Hercules, son of Zeus and Alcmene. Hercules was said to have raped and killed Evander's daughter, who was later laid to rest on the Palatine, but the Palatinians later forgave him when he vanquished the cannibalistic troll Cacus, who lived in a cave overlooking the neighboring Aventine Hill.

Evander was allegedly the predecessor to the Etruscan influence in Rome, as he was said to have been the first to bring the Greek laws, alphabet, and gods (collectively known as the "Pantheon") to Italian soil. Among the customs he brought with him from his homeland – such as reading and writing – was the festival of the *Lupercalia,* celebrated in honor of the fertility god, Lupercus. The *Lupercalia* was originally created as a convention of sorts for shepherds looking to sweeten their chances of breeding. This festival, later adopted by the Romans, became one of, if not the longest-lasting of all pagan observances. Celebrated on the 15th of every February, the festival was altered to extol Inuus, a horned deity of nature and sex who was part-god, part-*lupus* (wolf). The Roman rendition of the festival, which involved nude men slathered in oil dancing around a stack of sacrificial gifts dedicated to Inuus, commemorated the next fascinating chapter of the hill's tale of origin. When Evander passed on, a small altar was later erected in his honor on the Aventine.

The Palatine Hill would also be the central setting for the tale of Romulus and Remus, the former supposedly the very first king and founder of Ancient Rome. As it always is with age-old folklore, much of the story, down to the details of its conception, have been made hazy by time and the clashing versions presented by the innumerable writers that authored them. Some believe that the twins were conceived by Mars, the Roman god of war, and the mortal princess, Rhea Silvia, daughter of Numitor, the king of Alba Longa (a city by Alban Hill). Shortly before the disputed seed was injected into Rhea's womb, her uncle, Amulius, dethroned her father and seized his brother's crown. To safeguard his crown from those tempted to follow in his footsteps, he had all of Numitor's heirs executed.

Finally, the imprisoned Rhea was made a Vestal Virgin. These virgins were a syndicate of women whose patron mother was the goddess of the hearth and family, Vesta. Virgins not only vowed to refrain from all physical or carnal pleasures for life, they were tasked with fanning and maintaining the flames of a sacred fire. Thus, it would only be a matter of time before the authorities caught wind of the growing bulge in her belly. Exactly who it was that impregnated Rhea remains a matter of contention. As mentioned, some insisted that a frisky Mars, who was visiting Earth at the time, had seduced and bedded Rhea. Others speculated that Hercules might have been the mystery man. Then, there was Livy, who claimed that Rhea, having been violated by an unidentified mortal, was so ashamed of the rape that she cried "divine birth."

Whatever the case, Rhea, now a Vestal Virgin, was doomed, for virgins who failed to uphold their vows of celibacy were to be buried alive. After mulling it over, King Amulius, who wanted the cursed children gone but at the same time feared retaliation from the potentially paternal god, settled on middle ground. Rhea was thrown behind bars once more, and given an ultimatum that allowed her to choose the limited fates of her twins. They were to be buried alive, starved and exposed, or tossed into the Tiber River. Based on Amulius' logic, Alba Longa would be immune to the gods' wrath if the twins were to die in Mother Nature's hands.

Her hands tied, Rhea grudgingly selected the sentence with the highest probability of survival. She was allowed to name her sons, and after bidding them a quick goodbye, Amulius' servants ripped the wailing babies from her arms and stuffed them into a basket. Rather than hurl them into the tempestuous waters and leaving them to sink to the bottom, the consciences of the servants was said to have snuck up on them. Still, unwilling to prod another stick at the fully-woken and furious beast that was Amulius, the servants laid the basket delicately onto the river, watching helplessly as it drifted down the stream and out of sight.

Thankfully, the river god, Tibernus, had wised up to the attempted infanticide. He soothed the turbulent waters, and in time, the basket snagged onto a protruding branch by the foot of the Palatine. A female wolf known as the "*Lupercale,*" having sniffed their scent, crept out to the woods and discovered the basket. Intrigued, the *Lupercale* clamped her teeth around the handle and trotted back to its cave on the hill. She tended to the shaken, but otherwise unharmed twins, and nursed them with her milk as nearby woodpeckers collected berries amongst other treats for the hungry toddlers.

**An ancient statue depicting the wolf and the twins**

Months later, a shepherd and his wife, Faustulus and Acca Larentia, stumbled across the toddler twins, promptly fell in love with them, and brought them home to raise them as their own. The boys learned the ins and outs to the art of shepherding, and when they became teenagers, became sheep-herders themselves. One day, shepherds from Alba Longa wandered onto the Palatine Hill. The shepherds did not take kindly to the twins' kicking them out of their territory, and the alpha-male hostilities escalated to a full-blown scuffle. In the end, the boys failed to fend them off; even worse, they had captured Remus, and were now en route to see the king. The only silver lining was that Amulius, under the impression that the twins were long dead, failed to recognize the boys.

Romulus rounded up a gang of local shepherds as Remus presumably paced about in his cell, plotting his escape. In the stealth of the night, Romulus and his men marched towards Alba Longa and slunk into the tower where his brother was held captive. There, they subdued the guards and freed Remus. By the end of the chaotic rescue mission, King Amulius had fallen victim to Romulus' sword.

The twins may have ruled together if not for their cut-throat rivalry, which was just as strong as their brotherly bond. The citizens of Alba Longa offered them the crown, to which the twins politely rejected, for they thirsted for a challenge and hoped to create a powerful utopian city from scratch. Only, their grand visions did not line up, as Romulus fought to create a settlement on Palatine Hill, where the *Lupercale* had suckled them. The equally stubborn Remus, on the other hand, refused to budge from Aventine.

In the hopes of settling the squabble, the brothers agreed to an augury-off – whoever spotted more birds from the most sacred spots on their hills would be crowned the victor. Romulus claimed to have spotted 12 birds, whereas Remus counted only half that number. A smug Romulus puffed out his chest, but before he could do much else, Remus crossed his arms and declared himself the victor, arguing that he had seen his flock first. Unable to resolve the stalemate, the brothers parted ways and set out to establish their settlements on their respective hills, muttering bitterly along the way.

Romulus's first order of business was to order the construction of a wall and trench fencing in Palatine Hill. He eventually extended his walls to surround the Capitoline and Quirinal Hills, and later kings carried on the project and stretched the defensive borders across the Aventine and Caelian Hills, and under King Servius, to the Esquiline and Viminal Hills. Plutarch, Tacitus, and other ancient historians have described Romulus's fortifications as a simple, but effective "4-sided" set of walls, but not much else is known about them. These defensive walls proved fruitful when it came to staving off most potential attackers, but they only functioned as "physical boundaries." *Pomerium*, an Etruscan invention, which directly translates into "post wall," were so-called "formal boundaries" in the shape of marble slabs, or *"cippi,"* that identified these borders and the dimensions of the inner territories. The oldest known *pomerium* was supposedly installed by Romulus himself on the edge of Palatine Hill. These slabs multiplied as more sections were tacked onto the walls over the years. Anyone bearing weapons – even military officials – were turned away at the *pomerium*. Not even sovereigns were entitled to surpass the *pomerium* without a sanctioned escort.

Rather than let bygones be bygones and devote his efforts to building a comparable city of his own, Remus continued to harass his brother, and mocked his walls. On one occasion, Remus had been so keen on aggravating his twin that he leaped over the border in the middle of construction. Some say Remus lost his footing and slipped, snapping his neck upon his bad landing. In St. Jerome's version of events, a cackling Remus landed on his feet and frightened off the laborers, but he was later killed via a spade to his head by one of Romulus' radical admirers. However, most interpretations of the story have Romulus confronting his brother and throttling him to death on the spot. A remorseful Romulus buried his brother that same week with an extravagant send-off. With Remus out of the picture, Romulus christened his city "Rome," and his walls reintroduced as the "Square of Rome." 753 BCE has since been immortalized as the birth year of the Eternal City.

After Romulus had booted out the previous authorities, the hill's Arcadian residents were joined by a sudden spike of exiles, former criminals, escaped slaves, and other "dregs" of society seeking a new lease on life. With the male-to-female ratio severely unbalanced, the Romans on Palatine Hill had trouble spawning the next generation. To remedy this problem, the men, under Romulus's orders, kidnapped Latin and Sabine women from nearby hills, raping them and intimidating them into marriage. Latin and Sabine forces later attempted to retrieve the unarmed women, but they were defeated by Romulus' forces. This is now considered the first ever victory for Rome.

As gripping as the legend is, modern historians agree that it is mere legend. While the tale of a pair of feuding twins raised by wolves had all the elements of a bestseller, the origin story discussed above is most likely much closer to fact. Other historians believe that the term "*lupa*" might have been lost in translation, for the word also meant "prostitute." The same skeptics have suggested that, going against popular belief, the twins might have actually been fostered by a streetwalker, rather than a she-wolf. The *lupanar*, or cave in which the boys were raised in may have also been slang for a brothel. As a side note, other historians have also suggested that the city's name might have been derived from the archaic term for the Tiber River, which was "*Rumon.*"

Bearing all this in mind, archaeologists on Palatine Hill made a striking discovery in 2007. They unearthed what they believed might have been the said cave. Upon lowering their camera into a crevice on the roof of the "vaulted cavern" over 50 feet below ground, the bug-eyed scientists marveled at the rainbow of mosaics and dusty altars on their feed. They had found a shrine devoted to the *Lupercale,* leading some to argue that this more than hints at the truthfulness of the legend.

Regardless, by the time Rome had evolved into an empire, Palatine Hill was a far cry from the fledgling and unsophisticated settlement it once was. Years before the arrival of Romulus or Evander, the very first peasants who claimed the hill were operating under an entirely different tune. The messy assemblage of men consecrated the hill by kindling a fire out of brushwood and hurdling across the roaring flames, which was said to "cleanse them of evil." The man who came out on the other end with the least burns inflicted upon him was chosen as the village head. He then attached a plow to a blessed bull and ushered the animal around the hill to mark their territory. In an era before set currencies, the peasants, who mostly earned their livings as cobblers, tailors, and bakers, bartered for essentials by exchanging metal tools, leather goods, fruits, vegetables, dairy, and wool.

Under the republic, a proper structure of government became fully realized for the first time. In addition to the consuls, all limited to a one-year term, Roman citizens elected the city-state's magistrates and tax collectors. The Senate had now blown up to a membership of 600. Up to 10 branches of the "Tribunes of the People," a committee founded to handle the affairs of the lower classes, were also introduced.

During this time, the wealthiest families in all the land set their sights on Palatine Hill, drawn to its breathtaking views, abundance of fresh air, and the cool, crisp weather during the summertime. As an added bonus, they were miles away from the squalid conditions and jarring sounds of chariot traffic on the streets that the residents of low-lying grounds had no choice but to endure. Here, they tore down the old clay huts and began to erect a series of beautiful villas and vacation homes filled with lavish courtyards and babbling fountains.

As the territories under the republic swiftly expanded, those in the government began to campaign for autocratic rule. They proposed to restore the monarchy and take the reins as the republic's emperor. This, they argued, would eliminate all stalling and inaction of legislation often caused by bickering officials. The emperor could cut out the middleman when needed, not only accelerating their growth, but cementing their status as a legitimate empire. Julius Caesar was among the first to promote the cause, but his endeavors came to a stop when he was assassinated by a traditionalist cabal of conspirators. Eventually, Caesar's adopted heir, Octavian, won the people over, and he left his stamp on history as the first emperor of the Roman Empire.

**Gautier Poupeau's picture of a bust of Caesar**

**A statue of Augustus**

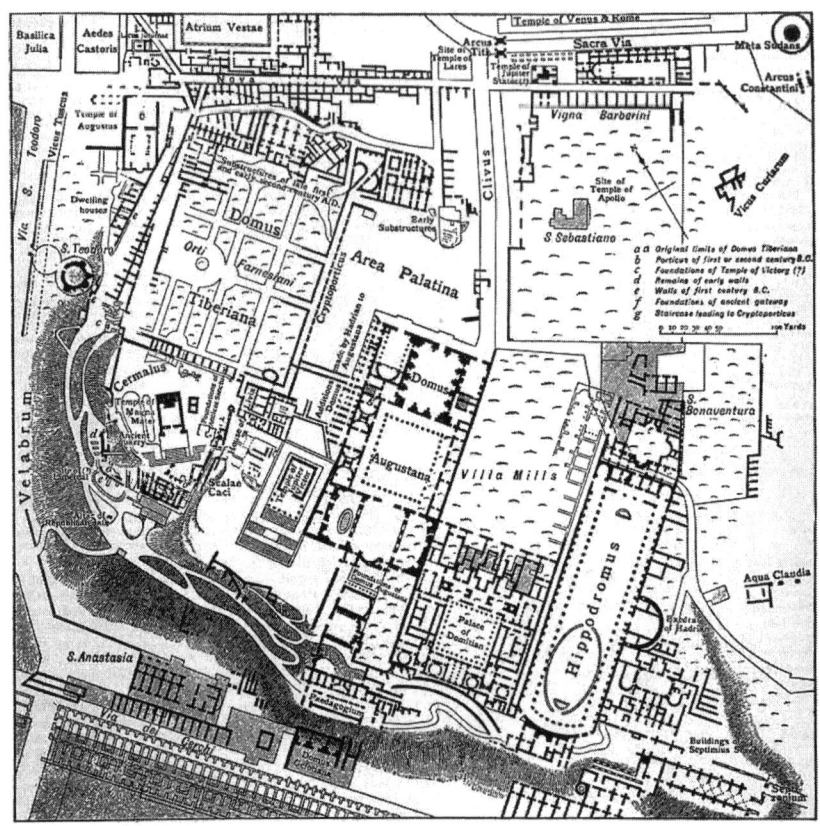

**A blueprint of Palatine Hill**

Emperor Augustus, who was born on the Palatine Hill, decided to build his imperial residence in Rome's aristocratic center. The House of Augustus, which rests on the pinnacle of the hill, was built in association with the emperor's patron deity, Apollo, in mind, and was an architectural marvel of its time. The Temple of Apollo, which was built next to the emperor's villa, has since vanished.

Vibrant frescoes featuring theatrical masks, pine branches, and elegant swans adorned the walls of the 2-story villa. The emperor's study was the most ornate of the rooms, with hulking satyrs (goat-men hybrids from Roman mythology), alluring winged females, and vine patterns on all 4 walls. When he could not bear the heat in his bedchambers during the worst days of the summer, he slept by the fountain in his courtyard as his servants fanned him with palm leaves throughout the night.

**One of the frescoes in the House of Augustus**

The emperors succeeding Augustus followed suit and built their homes on the Palatine Hill, enlarging the square of imperial residences, which came to be known as the *Domus Tiberiana*, after Emperor Tiberius. The ground around the complex was flattened to magnify the courtyard. That also made it easy to install a chain of underground walkways connecting the palace to safe bases on nearby hills. The walls of these secret passages were decorated with frescoes of a similar theme, too.

**Some of the ruins of the Domus Tiberiana**

Emperor Domitian was one of the chief renovators of the imperial square. He commissioned laborers to repave the steps up the Palatine, known as the *"Scala Caci"* (Cacus' steps), and to construct the *Clivus Palatinus*, a road that led to the palaces. Later, he added the *Domus Flavia*, its main feature the peristyle, which was a "columned porch" encircling a garden that was used to entertain visitors and advisers; as well as the Stadium of Domitian, his very own racecourse.

Interest in the hill waned until it was struck by a resurgence during the Renaissance. Property values skyrocketed, which prompted the arrival of a new batch of Italian nobles. In 1550, Cardinal Alessandro Farnese purchased a plot of land on the Palatine, which he transformed into the first private botanical gardens in Europe. The Farense garden was home to all kinds of artwork, a sanctuary for birds, and a *nymphaeum* (a sacred monument built for the water nymphs).

**Farnese**

When the public's boredom with the hill returned after the Renaissance, the gardens, as well as most of the hill, crumbled into disuse and were left neglected until the Palatine was turned into an archaeological site. Today, some 4 million tourists make the hike up to the Palatine peak, all for a gander at the Colosseum, the home of the gladiators.

## Aventine

"Quanta Roma fuit, ipsa ruina docet (the ruins of Rome spell its past greatness)." – Hildebert of Lavardin, 12th century bishop

In the 7th century BCE, King Ancus Marcius traced the outlines of Aventine territory for the first time by lengthening the walls to cut across the valley floor between the Aventine and Caelian Hills. The fortified boundaries helped smoothen the king's nerves, but those who ridiculed the paranoid king had to swallow their words when the walls kept the settlement intact during an unexpected attack. A ditch fortification called the "*Fossa Quiritium*" was later added to create another obstacle for would-be intruders.

A small section of the Caelian Hill, as well as all of Janiculum, stood behind the defensive walls, and thus belonged to Aventine property. If one were to scan the texts written by authors under Marcius' reign, the hill was depicted as a tiny paradise "wooded with trees of all kinds" with lovely laurels (fragrant evergreen shrubs) aplenty. While there remains a spot on the hill today known to the locals as "The Laurels," most of the bushes have disappeared, and the tract of land modernized with new buildings, as well as the preserved temple of Diana.

The *Pons Sublicius*, the earliest known bridge in Rome, arched over the Tiber River, linking Janiculum to the hill. It was constructed entirely out of wood, for this was built in a time before the Romans had a thorough understanding of metallurgy. The bridge was later placed under papal care, but all the prayers and blessings could not save the bridge from its shoddy workmanship.

Over the years, many brave enough to make the trek across the *Pons* had the wind knocked out of them when gnarly waves flooded the overpass. Those who heard the chilling, undeniable crack of the wobbly bridge dove headfirst into the water, lest they injure themselves further by going down with the collapsing structure. To the Romans at Aventine Hill, these were black omens from the gods (known as *prodigium*) disguised as accidents; deities were either warning the people about an impending disaster, or punishing them for a moral misdeed. Nonetheless, authorities repaired the bridge again and again, and the structure persevered until the 5th century AD.

Apart from its alleged beginnings as Remus's place of dwelling, the Aventine Hill, located in the southern end of the range, rose to prominence in the public eye as the official "plebeian hill" of Rome. Some say it was the mythological rivalry between Romulus and Remus that drove a rift between the patrician and plebeian classes, which widened sometime in the 5th century BCE. When Rome entered what is now referred to as the "Late Republic" period, the Palatine had become synonymous with the rich, and the Aventine was associated with the cultist plebeians of the working class.

The Aventine Triad, a term for the cult of Liber, Libera, and Ceres, the gods of harvest and fertility, came to fruition in 493 BCE, shortly after the fall of the first monarchy and Rome's transition into a republic. The triad was founded in the *templum*, a patch of hallowed ground on the Aventine Hill.

Those in the upper echelons of society had looked down on the plebeians from the start. Though the majority of the population comprised the working class, to the patricians, the plebeians were nothing more than unworldly, overly religious simpletons. On the contrary, the plebeians were the fuel that kept the city running, for the name pertained to the laborers, merchants, wine-makers, importers, exporters, and guilds of skilled craftsmen and artisans.

When Roman aristocrats continued to snub the waving arms of the plebeians, and awarded coveted positions in political, religious, and military offices to often less qualified patricians, the city's commoners would stand for it no longer.

Particularly in times of famine or whenever their services were needed the most, Roman peasants staged a *secessio plebis*, or "withdrawal of the commoners," one of the earliest known cases of an organized protest. Only, in lieu of mass sit-ins or picket-sign chanting, hordes of plebeians simply closed the doors to all their places of business and made themselves scarce, essentially sending all daily transactions grinding to a halt. As all food and essentials were held hostage by the plebeians, the disgruntled aristocracy would be left with no other alternative but to yield to their demands.

The ongoing tension, wrestle for power, and fight for equality that resulted from the opposite classes is now remembered as the "Struggle of the Orders," one that began circa 494 and dragged on until 287 BCE. There were said to have been a total of 5 secessions within this length of time. The struggle is also believed to have molded and contributed to the decreeing of new laws in later developments of the Roman constitution.

In 456 BCE, a tribunician law wordily titled the "*lex icilia de aventino publicando*," permanently bestowed ownership and semi-dominion of the Aventine Hill upon the plebeians, officially classifying the area "*ager publicus*" (public land). Aulus Regillensis, the Roman dictator at the time, funded the construction of a new temple on the hill reserved for the triad, which faced the Circus Maximus. The first *ludi scaenici* (religious dramas) were also said to have been performed in this temple. On top of the temple built by Regillensis, places of worship constructed for Diana, Minerva, and Juno. Regardless of their differences, under the *Lex Canuleia*, a law issued 11 years later due to public demand, patricians and plebeians who had fallen for one another were permitted to sanctify their union with the sacrament of marriage.

Professor Giuseppina Maria Oliviero elaborated on the importance of the plebeian-friendly laws: "The political and economic value of the lex...publicando constitutes a turning point in the plebeian struggle: thanks to this law, not only did the plebeians have soil where they might build their houses, but the Aventine began to represent a typically plebeian quarter, a political and religious center of the plebeian community..."

With a territory to claim as their own, the plebeians drew up their own constitution and elected their own officials, which formed the Plebeian Tribunes. They gave the patricians a taste of their own medicine by banning them from all assemblies. They, too, consulted a variant form of augury, designed by Marsyas, a close companion of Liber. Anyone who dared defy the plebeian laws was vilified as "*homo sacer*," executed, and had their property seized.

As the hill was technically situated outside the *pomerium* until Claudius's rule in the mid-1st century CE, the hill became a magnet for unorthodox cults that revered deities outside of the

Roman pantheon, and were therefore, banned from operating within the city limits. When Rome remodeled itself as an empire, new mystery religions worshiping more Roman deities popped up along the Aventine. In the early years of the 2nd century CE, a temple was built for the cult of Jupiter Dolichenus, a brotherhood that bore a roster of up to 260 devotees at one time. Another shrine devoted to the Persian sun god, Mithras, was constructed by its cult later that century. Around this time, a sanctuary for a cult that honored Isis was also founded where the Basilica of Santa Sabina now stands.

**D. Nalor's picture of the Basilica of Santa Sabina**

The hill was virtually void of any patrician presence after the publishing of the *lex publicando*, but by the time Rome entered the imperial age, the hill was converted to a primarily aristocratic neighborhood. A few emperors were also said to have lived here for a time, such as Emperor Trajan, and his closest comrade, Licinius Sura. The *Thermae Suranae*, otherwise known by its alternative moniker, the "Baths of Licinius Sura," was built for the influential senator on the peak of the hill.

# Capitoline

"And in a short while, the generation of living creatures are changed, and like runners, relay the torch of life." – attributed to Lucretius, a Roman poet from the 1st century BCE

Long before the Capitoline, or *Campidoglio* Hill, earned its prestige as the political and religious hub of Rome, the knoll was populated by the Sabine people. Sabine vagabonds are said to have chanced across the space sometime during the Iron Age. They occupied the higher regions of the hill, which at one point fell under the jurisdiction of the Sabine community on the Quirinal Hill, whereas Romulus and his men took control of the lower-lying regions. The Capitoline's geographical advantages made the hill one of the most desirable places to colonize, for it stood right by the ford of the Tiber River, the turnpike by King Servius's walls. Even better, the hill's steep and cragged sides was an ideal natural deterrent to those unwelcome in Capitoline territory.

There were 2 summits on the *Campidoglio*, the smallest of the 7 hills – the *Arx*, a higher, but narrower apex, which sits to the north; and on the south, the *Capitolium*, which was lower and wider in girth. The sunken belt of land wedged between the pair of summits was nicknamed the "Asylum," which served as an underground foxhole for refugees and defectors. It was supposedly Romulus himself who had placed a label on the zone when he was on the hunt for new colonists. This became a "designated point of arrival" for new immigrants who had hopped onto the other side in search of greener grass. It was when Romulus failed to recruit enough men that he resorted to seizing the Sabine women on the Capitoline and Quirinal Hills.

Centuries before the hill won its sobriquet, the *"Caput Mundi"* (the head of the world), the very mention of the *Campidoglio* was enough to stir every last hair on one's arms. Ancient Romans before the Republic went out of their way to avoid speaking its dreaded name, and if it was spoken, it was said in a quavering whisper so quiet it would not wake a mouse. This was the *Mons Tarpeius*, or in English, the "Tarpeian Rock." The notorious Tarpeian Rock was not a rock per se, but a rounded, almost semi-disc shaped cliff that hovered up to 75 feet off the ground on the southern neck of the hill. Yet another myth tells the story behind its etymology.

**A modern picture of the site of the Tarpeian Rock**

At the center of this cautionary tale is the Roman heroine and Vestal Virgin Tarpeia. Tarpeia, the daughter of Sprius Tarpeius, who was the commander of the Capitoline fortress under Romulus. During the war that erupted following the Roman rape of the Sabine women, the desperate Sabine forces, who were determined to eject all Romans from the hill, decided to appeal to Tarpeia for aid. The initially tentative Tarpeia declined, but when a precious chest bursting with glittering jewelry and other gilded accessories was shoved under her nose, the greedy maiden was swayed. In the wee hours of the next evening, Tarpeia stole out of her home and unhitched the lock of the city's front gates, the jewel-studded bracelets wrapped around her arms winking in the dark of the night.

Just as expected, Sabine soldiers sidled through the crack of the gate just hours later. Unbeknownst to the Sabines, the Roman guards had been tipped off by Tarpeia, and had concealed themselves in the bushes, ready to pounce at any moment. Nonetheless, the Roman guards failed to curb the Sabines. Once they were aware of Tarpeia's attempted trickery, they nabbed her and "crushed her with their shields." According to other storytellers, when the Sabines realized that they could not trust someone who would double-cross their own kind,

Tarpeia was rammed off the said cliff, kicking off the gruesome tradition.

From that point forward, all murderers, perjurers, traitors, and "larcenous slaves" were launched off the rock. A fraction of the condemned were those that suffered from mental or "severe" physical disabilities, for they were believed to have incurred the ire of the gods, and as such, deserved to be put to death. To some, the shame attached to the death by Tarpeian Rock was a "fate worse than death," as those dragged to the cliff were guilty of the most unthinkable crimes.

The Mamertine Prison, or the *Carcere Mamertino*, which sat on the foot of the hill, was yet another feared landmark of the Capitoline. Built sometime in the 7$^{th}$ century BCE by King Marcius, the Mamertine was the only prison in all of Rome. Notwithstanding its name, the Mamertine resembled a dungeon more than it did a prison. Instead of individual cells stacked on top of one another in some rusty building, the Mamertine started out as 2 large holes burrowed under the city sewers, roughly 12 feet underground, with only a manhole-sized hole in the center of these vaulted ceilings for detainees to slither in and out of. Those awaiting their execution were said to have been packed into these filthy quarters like a box of crayons; the dungeons were later merged into one, but even then, only measured 6.5 feet in height and 22 feet across.

The underground dungeon of Mamertine was called the "Tullianum," named after that who envisaged it, Servius Tullius. The ground-floor of the prison was built in the form of a trapezoid, and like its neighboring structures, was constructed out of *tufa* blocks. *Tufa* was a coarser, but more malleable type of limestone found in volcanic deposits all over Italy.

Another shallow hole was dug in the middle of the dirt-caked stone floors for the prisoners to urinate or defecate in. The bathroom was almost never emptied, so it was prone to excessive spillage at times the prison was pushing maximum capacity, which was more often than not. An iron door secured with heavy-duty locks stood on the far end of the chamber, which led to the city's official sewer system, the *Cloaca Maxima*. Prisoners who perished before their execution dates – mostly due to starvation – were chucked out the door with no second thought.

A number of those who lost their lives in the grimy cell were political prisoners and prisoners of war. Among the famous figures said to have done time in Mamertine are Simon bar Giora, who led an insurgency in Judea during the First Jewish-Roman War, and Vercingetorix, the Gallic leader who marshaled the Gauls together in an unsuccessful revolt against Caesar. The most memorable names on the list, however, belonged to Christ's apostles, Paul and Peter. The Church of San Giuseppe dei Falegnami was later built directly on top of the Mamertine. Its prison, which can be found in the basement, has been restored, and now welcomes visitors from around the globe. A marble plaque, which has faded to a shade of taupe, has since been mounted onto the east wall of the prison, with a list of the saints and martyrs that are believed to have graced the premises with their presence carved onto it.

**The site today**

A separate plaque names other notable prisoners, as well as their causes of death. To the back of the dungeon-slash-museum stands an altar illuminated by candles with the wreathed busts of Saints Paul and Peter in its center. Above the altar is a stone tile featuring the alleged impression of St. Peter's head, from where his bleeding head had left a mark on the floor when he was flung into the dungeon.

In contrast to the Aventine Hill, the cultist capital of the land, the Capitoline bore a long-held reputation for being the official sacred mount under the Roman crown. Plainly put, most of the temples erected on the Capitoline were dedicated to deities who were classed under the traditional Roman pantheon. The most illustrious of all the pagan temples on the *Campidoglio* was the Temple of Jupiter Optimus Maximus, perched on top of the summit of the *Capitolium* for maximum visibility. At one point in time, it was known to have been the most highly revered place of worship in Italy. Built by Tarquinius Priscus, the first Etruscan-born king of Rome, the deluxe temple towered over the nearby structures at over 173 feet in height, its spacious body measuring about 207 feet from one wall to the other.

**A speculative model of the temple**

In spite of what its name suggests, the temple was consecrated to not just Jupiter, but a trio of gods, including Juno Regina and Minerva. The main hall was split into 3 *cellae,* or rooms, reserved for each deity. Under the dripping bristles of the paintbrush, the temple exterior is usually portrayed as a grand structure with a wide, sloping roof built out of pure gold, shored up by dozens of slender white columns.

Following its first round of construction, a few intricately crafted terracotta *acroteria* – ornamental medallions or sculptures featuring headshots of the deities or mythological beasts – were fixed onto the sides of the temple's roofline. Roosted on the middle of the roof was a life-sized statue of Jupiter behind a 4-horsed chariot, also sculpted out of terracotta. Jupiter's face was painted blood-red, which began another longstanding custom that saw Roman generals shimmying up the backs of statues to splash the faces of the war gods in red to commemorate a victory on the battlefield.

Ironically, the most sacred ground in all of Rome was also among the most cursed. The temple burned down and had to be both partially and completely rebuilt more than 3 times, at least twice because of lightning strikes. The terracotta statue of Jupiter was replaced twice, one in gold and the other in ivory. Jupiter was later flanked by the similarly-sized statues of Minerva and Juno Regina. The final version of the temple, which was rebuilt by Emperor Domitian, held on until it was pillaged by the Vandals.

Before its demise, this was the setting for all consul elections under the Republic, which was held every 13th of September. On the 1st of January, the fresh elects gathered at the temple for an opulent induction ceremony. The rest of the year, the temple was used for a variety of religious festivals. On the Ides (the 15th or 16th) of each month, a meaty white sheep was gutted and placed on the altar for Jupiter. On the feast day of Jupiter, which fell on the Ides of every September, the Capitoline community patiently queued to present their offerings to all 3 deities. The sacrificial ceremony was followed by a colorful banquet starring roasted drumsticks, garden vegetables, and a medley of the sweetest fruits.

Another prominent place of worship was the Temple of Juno Moneta, which sat on the *Arx*. This was a former fortress refashioned into a temple in 344 BCE by the city's then-general, Marcus Camillus, in the hopes of gaining the god's favor during wartime. The word "*Moneta*" stems from "*monere,*" the Latin term for "warning." The official mint of Rome, or the "*ad monetam*," stood next to the temple, which may be the paternal term for "money."

As the story goes, one fateful day, priests and laymen passing by the temple heard strange voices from within. With cocked eyebrows, they ducked into the temple to investigate. When they could not find its source, the Romans, on the verge of calling it a day, heard the ghostly, disembodied voices once again. This time, its message of an imminent earthquake was crystal clear. Those who heard the voices would have shrugged it off as a prank, but lo and behold, the temple was devastated by a violent earthquake just a few days later, just as the voices had predicted.

Others say that the "*moneta*" part of the temple's name harks back to the time a heaven-sent flight of geese soared over the Capitoline, their deafening honks alerting the Romans of the approaching Gaul invaders en route to the *Campidoglio*. From then on out, the villagers gifted sacrificial offerings to the "holy geese" on a marked date of the calendar each year. The hounds specifically trained as guard dogs were kicked off the Tarpeian Rock.

What came to be called the "Capitoline Games" was also founded to eternalize their defeat of the Gauls. Known as "*Pentathlum*" in Latin, the games featured a line-up of chariot races and gymnastics-oriented competitions, as well as sing-offs and other musical contests.

Another beacon of the hill was the *Tabularium*, which was built on the plot of land between the Temples of Juno and Jupiter. The 2 lower floors of the enormous 4-story structure featured a plain *tufa*-brick with a gaping rectangle for a door. The upper levels of the sandy-gold building consisted of an open-aired colonnade of 11 arches, and a b-shaped roof tiled in rusty-red. The *Tabularium* functioned as the official State archives, its library stocked with papyrus scrolls and wax tablets of deeds, treaties, laws, and proclamations, and perhaps even a trove of top-secret documents.

**A picture of the ruins of the *Tabularium***

During the years of the Avignon papacy, when the papal office was relocated to France, the number of Capitoline residents dwindled. Huge sections of the hill were turned into goat pastures for nearby shepherds, and for a time, the Capitoline was referred to as the "*Monte Caprino*," or "goat mountain." Like the Palatine, the *Campidoglio* remained largely ignored until the Renaissance.

It was during this cultural golden age that the Capitoline complex underwent a major makeover. Holy Roman Emperor Charles V was said to have been so antagonized by the pitiful state of the place that he immediately put together a team to give the bedraggled area a much-needed touch-up. In 1536, Michelangelo was hired by Pope Paul III to design the *Piazza del Campidoglio*, a spectacular square of palazzos built in the Asylum pocket of the Capitoline. The piazza can be accessed by the *Cordonata*, a slow-rising stairwell with uniquely wide and smooth steps. A pair of lion statues made out of basalt can be found on the bottom of the steps, posted on either side of the stairwell.

**A picture of the *Piazza del Campidoglio***

## Esquiline

"Christianity has made a death of a terror which was unknown to the gay calmness of the Pagan." – Ouida, 19th century English novelist

Rome's transition from paganism to Catholicism was anything but a smooth ride. Plenty of events from the struggle between both parties is captured in the monuments sitting on the

Esquiline, the glorious green gem of a mound sitting between the Viminal and Caelian Hills. The Esquiline is home to 2 summits – the Cispian and Oppian peaks.

In mid-July of 64 CE, a terrible fire erupted in the shopping center close to the Circus Maximus, one of Rome's largest chariot stadiums. Despite the firefighters' best efforts, the flames raged on for 6 days, eventually spreading to the slums. The dry, wooden buildings and harsh gusts of winds acted as its accelerant, and by the time the flames were contained, nearly 67% of the city was nothing but rubble and debris, large chunks of which hid dozens of corpses. Among the casualties of the fire were the Temple of Jupiter Stator, the Atrium Vestae, and hundreds of Romans, while thousands wept over the scorched remnants of their homes.

**A bust of Nero**

What appears most likely is that the fire was an accident, likely caused by flammable materials near the Circus Maximus. Indeed, blazes of such kind were common until the 19th century, in overcrowded cities with wooden houses closely packed together, lit and heated by open flames and with no organized official fire brigades. Rome would suffer two more major fires in the next 15 years.

However, the grapevines were soon abuzz with rumors that Emperor Nero was the culprit.

Many speculated that it was his desperate attempt at snaking around the stifling senate so that he could renovate Rome as he so pleased. Though there was plenty of evidence to suggest that Nero was more than 35 miles away when the fire began, he opted for the easy way out by pointing his finger at the Christians. The secretive sect, which still boasted only small numbers but was fast growing in popularity, was viewed with suspicion and even hatred, as the Jews also were, by much of the Roman Empire. The main reason for this dislike was simple: the other pagan polytheistic traditions which flourished side by side throughout the empire might advocate the superiority of their own particular gods but, unlike the Christians, would not deny the existence of others. Christians flat-out believed that theirs was the only true God, and were not afraid to say so. Consequently, they were highly unpopular.

Nero capitalized on that unpopularity by accusing Christians of being responsible for the blaze, though it does not appear as though any motive was ever ascribed to them. Several were seized and, after being tortured, confessed (it is unclear whether they confessed to being Christians, or to the arson itself, but most sources are in accord in saying that they confessed *because* they were tortured). Scores of Christians were martyred, some draped in the skins of wild animals and then torn apart by dogs in the arena, others crucified in a mockery of Jesus's martyrdom, and still more were burned alive, nightly, to serve as illumination for Nero's garden banquets. The first institutionalised persecution of the Christians in the history of the Roman Empire (but not the last) had begun.

Tacitus described Nero's scapegoating of the Christians, writing, "Consequently, to get rid of the report, Nero fastened the guilt and inflicted the most exquisite tortures on a class hated for their abominations, called Christians by the populace. Christus, from whom the name had its origin, suffered the extreme penalty during the reign of Tiberius at the hands of one of our procurators, Pontius Pilatus, and a most mischievous superstition, thus checked for the moment, again broke out not only in Judaea, the first source of the evil, but even in Rome, where all things hideous and shameful from every part of the world find their centre and become popular. Accordingly, an arrest was first made of all who pleaded guilty; then, upon their information, an immense multitude was convicted, not so much of the crime of firing the city, as of hatred against mankind. Mockery of all sorts was added to their deaths. Covered with the skins of beasts, they were torn by dogs and perished, or were nailed to crosses, or were doomed to the flames and burnt, to serve as a nightly illumination, when daylight had expired."

The emperor reactivated the persecution of Christians and kicked it up to full throttle, adding fuel to the flames by escalating the propaganda against Christians. Many, if not all, of these "superstitious" fiends, Nero asserted, were bloodthirsty cannibals, for they partook in the sacrament of the Eucharist, wherein they ingested the "body of Christ." Others who learned about the Christian celebration of "agape," the biblical term for brotherly and platonic love, mistook them for orgy-powered festivals that promoted incest, promiscuity, and other debauchery. A little clarification was all it would have taken to set things straight, but the rumors about the Jesus-loving folk stuck.

At the same time, Nero took advantage of the fire to quickly build the *Domus Aurea*, the extraordinary imperial residence on the Esquiline, which ran from the Oppian peak to the Palatine. Historian Eric Varner concisely sums up the grumbling public's sentiments: "They would have been happy if Nero had built the *Domus Aurea* out in the country, but to do it here in the city really was an extraordinary kind of statement."

If one was to take a tour through the *Domus Aurea*, it would not be difficult to see precisely what it was that ticked off those left homeless. The grandeur practically emanating from the palace was said to have been so incredible that neither full-color paintings nor literary descriptions could do it justice. For starters, a triple porch that measured over a mile long bordered the immense premises. The courtyard, furnished with exotic flowers and greenery from as far as Asia Minor, was large enough to house a mammoth 120 foot statue of Nero. Next to the courtyard was a colossal "pool of water like a sea," accompanied by a set of complementary guest houses and handsome buildings. It would take more than week to complete the rest of the tour, for there were the cornfields, gardens, vineyards, and animal sanctuaries still to peruse.

The near-blinding interior of Nero's main palace was another showstopper in itself. The labyrinth of rooms featured dozens of banquet halls – with 50 just in the west wing – decked from its domed (and a few revolving) ceilings to its kaleidoscopic floors in shimmering gold, gems, and mother-of-pearl. Several of these rooms contained small, trickling marble fountains; other rooms had a musical stream of water cascading down the ivory panels of the walls. Giddy guests often went home with complimentary bouquets, as well as bottled perfumes made from these rare flowers. But as it turned out, the emperor's stupendous palace was never completed, and it lasted no more than 4 years.

Nero's decision to build his palace on the Esquiline might have been puzzling to some, considering the hill's less than appealing history as a necropolis. Before the Roman Empire rose from the ashes of the Republic, the east of the Esquiline was apportioned to the poor so that they could bury their dead, as burials within the city limits were prohibited. These graves for the poor were known as the "*puticuli*" (burial pits). At the time, the site also served as a landfill, meaning the patch of land must have been thronging with all sorts of insects. Still, the peasants swallowed their pride, making do with what they could afford. The corpses of criminals were also delivered here, but rather than head for the spade, laborers left their bodies on the cliffs for the birds to feast upon. Later, a cremation cemetery joined the funerary community on the hill.

Authorities outlawed the dumping of refuse on the Equiline sometime in the 3rd century BCE. Once the area was swept clean, a new burial ground filled with a clean grid of private tombs was introduced on the north of the Esquiline. This site was chartered by the Senate to those in the upper tiers of society, and when Catholicism dominated, heroes who died a noble death. The greatest episodes, as well as the last moments of the martyrs' lives, were memorialized in paintings and frescoes, as well as engraved inscriptions that decorated the monuments and headstones erected atop their graves.

Roman plebeians continued to lay their dead to rest on the southern stretch of the Esquiline. This area, called the *"commune sepulcrum,"* hosted wide, but shallow *puticuli* crammed with the misshapen corpses of the executed, as well as slaves, wayfarers, and others who could not cough up the sum for a grave of their own. During the Empire era, Emperor Augustus refilled the burial pits, and commanded for a hearty bed of earth to be laid on top of it. Here, he built the *Horti Maecenatis*, or "Gardens of Maecenas," a superb natural sanctuary filled with baths and libraries.

**A painting depicting the *Villa of Maecenas***

Standing on the topmost summit of the Esquiline is one of the 4 patriarchal churches, the Basilica of Santa Maria Maggiore, featuring a 246 foot bell tower with 5 fantastic brass bells, the tallest in all the land. Mother Mary herself was said to have been the muse behind the basilica. Legend has it that the Virgin Mother visited Pope Liberius in his slumber, and as his eyelids fluttered furiously, ordered him to construct a church in her name. Come daylight on the 5th of August, a mysterious shower of snow fell upon the hill on the Esquiline, the snowfall perfectly marking the dimensions of the basilica.

**Pierre-Selim Huard's picture of the Basilica of Santa Maria Maggiore**

## Quirinal, Caelian, and Viminal

"We are just statistics, born to consume resources." – Quintus Horatius Flaccus, lyric poet, "Epistles"

While the remaining 3 hills might not house as many memories, each adds its own flavor to the rich and multifaceted annals of Roman history.

The Quirinal Hill, the northernmost and tallest of all the *montes* on the *Septimontium,* was named after Quirinus, the pagan god of the Sabines who was believed to have settled there. Though Quirinus, a close relative of the Roman war god Mars, is widely considered the most "complex" of all the gods in the local pantheon, not a single myth about the deity is known to exist. Some believe that Quirinus is the godly form of Romulus. Whoever he was, Quirinus was one of the 3 gods who hosted a brand of *flamen,* a name assigned to pagan priests.

In 325 BCE, a temple was constructed in honor of Quirinus on the main crest of the hill. Ovid, the Roman poet, was one of many robbed of their breaths upon their visits to the temple. The splendid place of worship lived amidst a thicket of trees, nestled comfortably under its cool shade. Pliny the Elder often retold the story regarding the pair of hallowed myrtle trees planted by the entrance of the temple, one dedicated to the patricians of Rome and the other to the plebeians. Whenever the patricians were propelled to the head of the race during the years of the Struggle, their plant was said to have thrived, whereas the plebeian's plant withered, and vice versa.

The temple was put under multiple renovations during the Republic, until it was rebuilt for the final time by Emperor Augustus, who was said to have greatly admired Romulus. The new and improved temple was braced by 76 columns, supposedly a forecast of the total number of years the emperor would live. This prediction proved to be accurate.

From the 1500s onwards, the Quirinal Hill was bracketed with aristocratic territory. Like those on the Palatine, Romans fought for a place on the highest lands of the Quirinal, hoping to avoid the dirty, noise-polluted streets below. Today, the *Palazzo del Quirinale,* or the "Quirinal Palace," a true testament to the wealth of the region, remains the leading highlight on the hill.

**The palace courtyard**

The palazzo, home to 4 Italian kings, 30 popes, and 11 presidents of the Republic of Italy, is the 6th largest palace in the world. Originally the summer getaway for Pope Gregory XIII in the late 16th century, who also wanted a break from the torturous humidity and daily rackets below, the 12,000-room palace now serves as a meeting point for the president and foreign leaders. Next to the palazzo are the Quirinal Gardens, colored with an abundance of flamboyant greenery, spanning over 4-hectares in size.

Formerly dubbed the "*Mons Querquetulanus*" after its distinctive oak forests, the Caelian Hill stood on the southeast of the *Septimontium* range. Chroniclers believe that the name of the hill was inspired by one of the greatest Roman warlords of all time, one with an unbeatable record – an Etruscan native by the name of Caelius Vibenna. Some of its first residents were those who had previously lived in Alba Longa but were transferred to the Caelian by King Tullus Hostilius when the city's borders were erased. The Caelian community eventually exploded, and it was divided by an invisible border that segregated the homes of the wealthy from those of the poor – not that one had any trouble telling these abodes apart. The rich lived in houses called "*domus*" – with over 2,000 of them built in the 300s. Classical author Olympiodorus of Thebes described these homes: "Each one of [them] had as many things inside it as a small town might have: a horse racing track, plazas, small temples, and various baths...One house could be a city."

Meanwhile, the less-affluent found shelter in "*insulae*," characterized by multiple floors that housed multiple families. These were essentially some of the world's first apartment buildings. By the 4$^{th}$ century, there were more than 45,000 *insulae* around Rome, squeezed between commercial buildings, workshops, and warehouses alike.

Apart from the Basilica of St. John Lateran, another of the quartet of papal churches, millions of visitors flock to see the *Thermae Antoninianae,* or the "Baths of Caracalla," every year. Over 13,000 Scottish prisoners of war were rounded up, and charged with evening out the land and dismantling the foundations of previous buildings. Another 6,000 or so specialty artisans and 600 marble workers also played an instrumental part in the workforce. All in all, it took at least 21,000,000 bricks to complete the project.

The Baths of Caracalla were easily one of the largest of its kind, for future successors expanded it with an extensive garden and park, a giant gymnasium, and a collection of diverse libraries. Its interior boasted marble walls and a stunning collection of frescoes and statues modeled after the Roman gods. Shards of marble and granite dipped in bright dye were carefully laid onto the mosaic-patterned floors, some featuring sea horses, fish, and other underwater creatures. A whimsical plaque erected by Tiberius Claudius remains on the site today, reading, "*Balnea, vina, Venus corrumpunt corpora nostra; sed vitam faciunt balnea, vina, Venus*" ("Baths, wine, and sex spoil our bodies; but baths, wine, and sex make up life.").

**Ethan Doyle White's picture of the ruins of the Baths of Caracalla**

Last, but certainly not least, was the Viminal Hill, or *"Collis Viminalis,"* the smallest on the *Septimontium* range. According to the timeline provided by 4th century historian Flavius Eutropius, the Viminal was the last of the *montes* to be included in the *Septimontium*. Before settlers began to camp out at the Viminal, the "steep" and "flat-topped" hill functioned as one of the main Servian fortresses.

The mound is believed to have been named after a cult devoted to Jupiter, whose members were among the earliest to occupy Viminal Hill. Others claim the Viminal received its name from the *vimina*, a dated term for willow trees that grew there.

Like those at Caelian Hill, most commoners lived in *insulae, but* Viminal apartments were half-residential and half-commercial; upper floors were reserved for living spaces, whereas butcheries, tailors, and other industrial spaces were found on the first floor.

The space nested in the valley between the Quirinal and the Viminal Hills was known to the locals as the "Subura." In the flat of the valley lived a crowded plethora of stalls, craftstores, and small factories. Under Caesar's rule, the Subura became the red-light district of Rome and the favorite rendezvous spot for immoral lovers, swarming with prostitutes, black market dealers, and other shady characters. Though spending a quiet afternoon in the hectic and grubby Subura was an impossible mission, the amount of animated life and energy provided a charm of its own.

Needless to say, the once barren hills of Rome have come a long way. Today, the ancient Romans wouldn't recognize the hills, which are dotted with sleek new buildings, immaculately restored structures, and pristinely preserved ruins. But at the end of the day, the legacy the 7 hills has left behind as the foundations of Rome is unchanging, and it will last for generations to come.

## Online Resources

Other books about ancient history by Charles River Editors

Other books about ancient Rome by Charles River Editors

Other books about the Seven Hills on Amazon

## Bibliography

Editors, US History. "6a. The Roman Republic." *US History: Ancient Civilizations*. Independence Hall Association in Philadelphia, 2008. Web. 18 July 2017. <http://www.ushistory.org/civ/6a.asp>.

Editors, Virtual Roma. "The City Walls." *Virtual Roma*. Virtual Roma, Ltd., 2011. Web. 18 July 2017. <http://roma.andreapollett.com/S4/walls.htm>.

Editors, Rachel's Rome Writings. "A Beginners' Guide to the Seven Hills of Rome." *Rachel's Rome Writings*. WordPress, 16 Jan. 2011. Web. 18 July 2017. <https://rachelsromewritings.com/2011/01/16/a-beginners%E2%80%99-guide-to-the-seven-hills-of-rome/>.

Gill, N. S. "The 7 Hills of Rome." *Thought Company*. Thought Company, Inc., 24 Apr. 2017. Web. 18 July 2017. <https://www.thoughtco.com/hills-of-rome-117759>.

Editors, Amazing Bible Timeline. "Rome, Walled 7 Hills of." *Amazing Bible Timeline*. Amazing Bible Timeline, LLC, 24 Nov. 2012. Web. 18 July 2017. <https://amazingbibletimeline.com/blog/walled-7-hills-of-rome/>.

Editors, Roman Empire. "The Founding of Rome." *Roman Empire*. Roman Empire.Net, 6 Apr. 2012. Web. 18 July 2017. <http://www.roman-empire.net/founding/found-index.html>.

Thayer, Bill. "THE SEPTIMONTIUM AND THE SEVEN HILLS." *University of Chicago Website*. Western Reserve University, Jan. 1906. Web. 18 July 2017. <http://penelope.uchicago.edu/Thayer/E/Journals/CP/1/1/Septimontium*.html>.

Editors, Rome Reborn. "Aventine Hill." *Rome Reborn*. University of Virginia, 2008. Web. 18 July 2017. <http://archive1.village.virginia.edu/spw4s/RomanForum/GoogleEarth/AK_GE/AK_HTML/GF-003.html>.

Editors, Rome Reborn. "Esquiline Hill." *Rome Reborn*. University of Virginia, 2008. Web. 18 July 2017. <http://romereborn.frischerconsulting.com/ge/GF-010.html>.

Editors, Welcome to Rome. "The Seven Hills of Rome." *Welcome to Rome*. Welcome to Rome, Ltd., 2009. Web. 18 July 2017. <http://www.welcometorome.net/en/about-rome/history/seven-hills>.

Editors, Time Maps. "Civilization: Etruscans." *Time Maps*. Time Maps, Ltd., 2017. Web. 18 July 2017. <https://www.timemaps.com/civilizations/etruscans/>.

Butler, Chris. "The Etruscans & their influence on Rome (c.800-500 BCE)." *Flow of History*. Chris Butler, 2007. Web. 18 July 2017. <http://www.flowofhistory.com/units/birth/4/FC27>.

Editors, Vatican.Va. "The Seven Hills of Rome." *Vatican.Va*. Internet Dominion Company, 27 June 2013. Web. 18 July 2017. <http://vatican.com/articles/rome/the_seven_hills_of_rome-a4131>.

Morey, William C., PhD. "Outlines of Roman History." *Forum Romanum*. Forum Romanum, LLC, 1909. Web. 18 July 2017. <http://www.forumromanum.org/history/morey01.html>.

Bedard, Moe. "The Umbri." *Gnostic Warrior*. Moe Bedard, 16 Sept. 2013. Web. 18 July 2017. <http://gnosticwarrior.com/umbri.html>.

Editors, Encyclopedia Britannica. "Latium." *Encyclopedia Britannica*. Encyclopedia Britannica, Inc., 11 May 2009. Web. 18 July 2017. <https://www.britannica.com/place/Latium>.

Cartwright, Mark. "Etruscan Trade." *Ancient History Encyclopedia*. Ancient History Encyclopedia, Ltd., 9 Feb. 2017. Web. 18 July 2017. <http://www.ancient.eu/article/1014/>.

Editors, Encyclopedia Britannica. "Fasces." *Encyclopedia Britannica*. Encyclopedia Britannica, Inc., 9 June 2017. Web. 18 July 2017. <https://www.britannica.com/topic/fasces>.

Platner, Samuel Ball. "Septimontium." *University of Chicago Website*. Oxford University Press, 1929. Web. 18 July 2017. <http://penelope.uchicago.edu/Thayer/E/Gazetteer/Places/Europe/Italy/Lazio/Roma/Rome/_Texts/PLATOP*/Septimontium.html>.

Sheldon, Natasha. "The Ludi Apollinares: Assimilating Greek Rites into Roman Religion." *Decoded Past*. WordPress, 8 July 2014. Web. 18 July 2017. <http://decodedpast.com/ludi-apollinares-assimilating-greek-rites-roman-religion/11248>.

Editors, Mysterious Etruscans. "The History of Etruria." *Mysterious Etruscans*. Mysterious Etruscans, Ltd., 1 Jan. 2006. Web. 18 July 2017. <http://www.mysteriousetruscans.com/history4.html>.

Editors, Encyclopedia Britannica. "Servius Tullius." *Encyclopedia Britannica*. Encyclopedia Britannica, Inc., 12 Aug. 2012. Web. 18 July 2017. <https://www.britannica.com/biography/Servius-Tullius>.

Clear, James. "Rome Wasn't Built in a Day, But They Were Laying Bricks Every Hour." *James Clear*. James Clear, 2017. Web. 18 July 2017. <http://jamesclear.com/lay-a-brick>.

Editors, Encyclopedia Britannica. "Evander." *Encyclopedia Britannica*. Encyclopedia Britannica, Inc., 8 Nov. 2007. Web. 19 July 2017. <https://www.britannica.com/topic/Evander>.

Editors, Roma Experience. "A GUIDE TO THE PALATINE HILL." *Roma Experience*. Roma Experience, Ltd., 2016. Web. 19 July 2017. <https://www.romaexperience.com/palatine-hill/#history>.

Editors, Encyclopedia Britannica. "Palatine Hill." *Encyclopedia Britannica*. Encyclopedia Britannica, Inc., 12 Aug. 2010. Web. 19 July 2017. <https://www.britannica.com/place/Palatine-Hill>.

Editors, Greek Mythology Wiki. "Evander of Pallene." *Greek Mythology Wiki*. MediaWiki, 2015. Web. 19 July 2017. <http://greekmythology.wikia.com/wiki/Evander_of_Pallene>.

Smith, William. "Lupercalia." *University of Chicago Website*. University of Chicago, 14 Feb. 2013. Web. 19 July 2017. <http://penelope.uchicago.edu/Thayer/e/roman/texts/secondary/smigra*/lupercalia.html>.

Gill, N. S. "The Roman Festival of Lupercalia." *Thought Company*. Thought Company, Inc., 15 Feb. 2017. Web. 19 July 2017. <https://www.thoughtco.com/the-roman-festival-of-lupercalia-121029>.

Editors, Revolvy. "Inuus ." *Revolvy*. Revolvy, LLC, 31 Mar. 2017. Web. 19 July 2017. <https://www.revolvy.com/main/index.php?s=Inuus&item_id=563719>.

Gill, N. S. "Romulus - Roman Mythology About the Founding and First King of Rome." *Thought Company*. Thought Company, Inc., 27 Feb. 2017. Web. 19 July 2017. <https://www.thoughtco.com/romulus-roman-mythology-119619>.

Trueman, C. N. "Romulus and Remus - History Learning Site." *The History Learning Site.* The History Learning Site, Ltd., 16 Mar. 2015. Web. 19 July 2017. <http://www.historylearningsite.co.uk/ancient-rome/romulus-and-remus/>.

Pitzer, Andrea. "Does a cave prove Romulus and Remus are no myth?" *USA Today 30.* USA Today, Inc., 6 Feb. 2008. Web. 19 July 2017. <https://usatoday30.usatoday.com/tech/science/discoveries/2008-02-06-romulus-remus-lupercale_n.htm>.

Garcia, Brittany. "Romulus and Remus." *Ancient History Encyclopedia.* Ancient History Encyclopedia, Ltd., 4 Oct. 2013. Web. 19 July 2017. <http://www.ancient.eu/Romulus_and_Remus/>.

Darling, David. "Rome, early history." *Internet Encyclopedia of History.* The Worlds of David Darling, 2016. Web. 19 July 2017. <http://www.daviddarling.info/encyclopedia_of_history/R/Rome_early_history.html>.

Editors, A View on Cities. "Palatine Hill." *A View on Cities.* A View on Cities, LLC, 2017. Web. 19 July 2017. <http://www.aviewoncities.com/rome/palatinehill.htm>.

Trueman, C. N. "How was Rome governed." *The History Learning Site.* The History Learning Site, Ltd., 16 Mar. 2015. Web. 19 July 2017. <http://www.historylearningsite.co.uk/ancient-rome/how-was-rome-governed/>.

Editors, Rome in the Footsteps. "On the Palatine Hill - Main Monuments." *Rome in the Footsteps of an XVIIIth Century Traveller.* Memoirs of Hadrian, 2007. Web. 20 July 2017. <https://www.romeartlover.it/Palatin1.html>.

Editors, Thought Eternity. "READ ABOUT THE INCREDIBILE STORY OF THE HOUSE OF AUGUSTUS AND LIVIA." *Thought Eternity.* Thought Eternity Tours, Ltd., 17 Mar. 2016. Web. 20 July 2017. <https://www.througheternity.com/en/blog/history/the-house-of-augustus-the-house-of-livia.html>.

Editors, World Monuments Fund. "House of Augustus." *World Monuments Fund.* World Monuments Watch, 2017. Web. 20 July 2017. <https://www.wmf.org/project/house-augustus>.

Editors, A View on Cities. "Aventine Hill." *A View on Cities.* A View on Cities, LLC, 2017. Web. 20 July 2017. <http://www.aviewoncities.com/rome/aventine.htm>.

Editors, Rome Archeomedia. "The Ancient Aventine..." *Rome Archeomedia.* Fondazione Ugo Burdoni, 2015. Web. 20 July 2017. <http://romearcheomedia.fub.it/aventino/storia.php?loc=en>.

Editors, Rome Reborn. "Aventine Hill." *Rome Reborn*. University of Virginia, 2008. Web. 20 July 2017. <http://romereborn.frischerconsulting.com/ge/GF-003.html>.

Editors, Revolvy. " Aventine Triad ." *Revolvy*. Revolvy, LLC, 20 June 2017. Web. 20 July 2017. <https://www.revolvy.com/main/index.php?s=Aventine%20Triad&item_type=topic>.

Editors, Wikipedia. "Secessio plebis." *Wikipedia*. MediaWiki, 29 Apr. 2017. Web. 20 July 2017. <https://en.wikipedia.org/wiki/Secessio_plebis>.

Editors, Wikipedia. "Conflict of the Orders." *Wikipedia*. MediaWiki, 3 June 2017. Web. 20 July 2017. <https://en.wikipedia.org/wiki/Conflict_of_the_Orders>.

Platner, Samuel Ball. "Pons Sublicius." *University of Chicago Website*. Oxford University Press, 25 July 2011. Web. 20 July 2017. <http://penelope.uchicago.edu/Thayer/E/Gazetteer/Places/Europe/Italy/Lazio/Roma/Rome/_Texts/PLATOP*/Pons_Sublicius.html>.

Editors, Info Please. "Capitoline Hill." *Info Please*. Sandbox Networks, Inc., 2012. Web. 20 July 2017. <https://www.infoplease.com/encyclopedia/history/ancient-greece-and-rome/ancient-history-rome/capitoline-hill>.

Editors, A View on Cities. "Capitoline Hill." *A View on Cities*. A View on Cities, LLC, 2017. Web. 20 July 2017. <http://www.aviewoncities.com/rome/capitolinehill.htm>.

Taul, Stephen. "Capitoline Hill: History, Architecture & Facts." *Study.Com*. Study.Com, 2014. Web. 20 July 2017. <http://study.com/academy/lesson/capitoline-hill-history-architecture-facts.html>.

Editors, Rome Reborn. "Capitoline Hill." *Rome Reborn*. University of Virginia, 2008. Web. 20 July 2017. <http://archive1.village.virginia.edu/spw4s/RomanForum/GoogleEarth/AK_GE/AK_HTML/GF-006.html>.

Editors, Famous Wonders. "Capitoline Hill." *Famous Wonders*. Famous Wonders, Ltd., 2015. Web. 20 July 2017. <http://famouswonders.com/capitoline-hill/>.

Editors, Ancient Origins. "The Infamous Mamertine Prison and the Supposed Incarceration of Saint Peter." *Ancient Origins*. Stella Novus, 19 July 2015. Web. 20 July 2017. <http://www.ancient-origins.net/ancient-places-europe/infamous-mamertine-prison-and-supposed-incarceration-saint-peter-003447>.

Bryant, Rae. "Roman Execution by Hurling From the Tarpeian Rock." *Thought Company*. Thought Company, Inc., 8 Feb. 2017. Web. 20 July 2017. <https://www.thoughtco.com/tarpeian-rock-roman-execution-121026>.

Editors, Wonderland 1981. "Tarpeian Rock – Infamous Execution Place for Traitors, Criminals and the Disabled." *Wonderland 1981*. WordPress, 19 Oct. 2012. Web. 20 July 2017. <https://wonderland1981.wordpress.com/2012/10/19/tarpeian-rock-infamous-execution-place-for-traitors-criminals-and-the-disabled/>.

Carr, K. E. "What is Tufa?" *Quatr US Study Guides*. Quatr, Inc., 2014. Web. 20 July 2017. <http://quatr.us/architecture/tufa.htm>.

Editors, Rome Reborn. "Temple of Jupiter Optimus Maximus." *Rome Reborn*. University of Virginia, 2008. Web. 21 July 2017. <http://romereborn.frischerconsulting.com/ge/TS-037.html>.

Findley, Andrew, PhD. "Temple of Jupiter Optimus Maximus, Rome." *Khan Academy*. Khan Academy Organization, 2015. Web. 21 July 2017. <https://www.khanacademy.org/humanities/ancient-art-civilizations/roman/roman-republic/a/jupiter-optimus-maximus>.

Editors, Piranesi in Rome. "Coins: the Temple through Time." *Piranesi in Rome*. Omeka, Inc., 2012. Web. 21 July 2017. <http://omeka.wellesley.edu/piranesi-rome/exhibits/show/temple-to-jupiter-optimus-maxi/coins-the-temple-through-time>.

Editors, Object Lessons. "Wax Tablet & Stylus, Ancient Rome, Replica." *Object Lessons*. New Opportunities Fund, 2016. Web. 21 July 2017. <https://www.objectlessons.org/childhood-and-games-romans/wax-tablet--stylus-ancient-rome-replica/s65/a1053/>.

Editors, A View on Cities. "Piazza del Campidoglio." *A View on Cities*. A View on Cities, LLC, 2017. Web. 21 July 2017. <http://www.aviewoncities.com/rome/piazzadelcampidoglio.htm>.

Editors, PBS. "The Great Fire of Rome Background." *PBS - Secrets of the Dead*. Thirteen Productions, LLC, 2014. Web. 21 July 2017. <http://www.pbs.org/wnet/secrets/great-fire-rome-background/1446/>.

Gurgone, Frederico. "Golden House of an Emperor." *Archaeology.Org*. Archaeological Institute of America, 10 Aug. 2015. Web. 21 July 2017. <http://www.archaeology.org/issues/187-1509/features/3562-golden-house-of-an-emperor>.

Cartwright, Mark. "Nero's Golden House." *Ancient History Encyclopedia*. Ancient History Encyclopedia, Ltd., 10 Mar. 2014. Web. 21 July 2017. <http://www.ancient.eu/article/661/>.

Editors, Rome Archeomedia. "Esquiline Necropolis." *Rome Archeomedia*. Fondazione Ugo Burdoni, 2014. Web. 21 July 2017. <http://www.romearcheomedia.it/esquilino/luoghi/index.php?page=esquilina&i=banner_necropoli&locc=esquilina&type=2&subtype=1&dove=Esquiline%20Necropolis>.

Editors, The Papal Basilica of Santa Maria Maggiore. " INSIDE THE BASILICA." *The Papal Basilica of Santa Maria Maggiore*. The Papal Basilica of Santa Maria Maggiore, 2006. Web. 21 July 2017. <http://www.vatican.va/various/basiliche/sm_maggiore/en/storia/interno.htm>.

Editors, Eyewitness to History. "Nero Persecutes the Christians, 64 A.D." *Eyewitness to History*. Ibis Communications, Inc., 2000. Web. 21 July 2017. <http://www.eyewitnesstohistory.com/christians.htm>.

Editors, Rome City Guide. "Quirinal Hill." *Rome City Guide*. Rome City Guide, Ltd., 2017. Web. 21 July 2017. <http://www.rome-city-guide.com/en/rome-attractions/seven-hills/quirinal-hill.html>.

Donati, Silvia. "The Quirinale Palace, Home of Italy's President." *Italy Magazine*. Bluespark, Ltd., 19 Jan. 2015. Web. 21 July 2017. <http://www.italymagazine.com/news/quirinale-palace-home-italys-president>.

Editors, Fandom. "Collis Viminalis - The Viminal Hill (Mons Aventinus)." *Fandom*. MediaWiki, 2011. Web. 21 July 2017. <http://monsaventinus.wikia.com/wiki/Collis_Viminalis_-_The_Viminal_Hill_(Mons_Aventinus)>.

Editors, Italian Ways. "ALL OF ROME LIVED IN THE CAELIAN HILL'S OLD HOUSES." *Italian Ways*. Italian Ways, Ltd., 2010. Web. 21 July 2017. <http://www.italianways.com/all-of-rome-lived-in-the-caelian-hills-old-houses/>.

Editors, Rome Reborn. "Caelian Hill." *Rome Reborn*. University of Virginia, 2008. Web. 21 July 2017. <http://romereborn.frischerconsulting.com/ge/GF-004.html>.

Editors, Livius.Org. "Rome, Baths of Caracalla." *Livius.Org*. Livius.Org, 1998. Web. 21 July 2017. <http://www.livius.org/articles/place/rome/rome-photos/rome-baths-of-caracalla/>.

Editors, Search Credo. " Quirinus (Roman deity)." *Search Credo*. Marshall Cavendish Corporation, 2012. Web. 21 July 2017. <https://search.credoreference.com/content/topic/quirinus_roman_deity>.

Editors, Rome Reborn. "Temple of Quirinus." *Rome Reborn*. University of Virginia, 2008. Web. 21 July 2017. <http://romereborn.frischerconsulting.com/ge/TS-052.html>.

Spiedel, Michael. *The Religion of Jupiter Dolichenus in the Roman Army*. N.p.: EPRO 63, 1978. Print.

Vout, Caroline. *The Hills of Rome: Signature of an Eternal City* . N.p.: Cambridge U Press, 2012. Print.

Mayo, Robert. *A New System of Mythology, in Two Volumes; Giving a Full Account of the Idolatry of the Pagan World*. N.p.: Palala Press, 2016. Print.

Gagarin, Michael. *The Oxford Encyclopedia of Ancient Greece and Rome: 7-Volume Set*. 1st ed. N.p.: Oxford U Press, 2009. Print.

Ovid. *Fastorum libri sex: The Fasti of Ovid*. Trans. James George Frazer. Vol. 1. N.p.: Cambridge U Press, 2015. Print. Cambridge Library Collection.

Pepin, Ronald E. *The Vatican Mythographers (Medieval Philosophy: Texts and Studies)*. 1st ed. N.p.: Fordham U Press, 2008. Print. Medieval Philosophy: Texts and Studies.

Mignone, Lisa. *The Republican Aventine and Rome's Social Order*. N.p.: U of Michigan Press, 2016. Print.

**Free Books by Charles River Editors**

We have brand new titles available for free most days of the week. To see which of our titles are currently free, click on this link.

## Discounted Books by Charles River Editors

We have titles at a discount price of just 99 cents everyday. To see which of our titles are currently 99 cents, click on this link.

Printed in Dunstable, United Kingdom